For: Emilie

From: Uncle Art & Aunt Chris

Thunder Bay Press
An imprint of Printers Row Publishing Group
10350 Barnes Canyon Road, Ste. 100, San Diego, CA 92121
www.thunderbaybooks.com

Text by Josephine Collins, copyright © Little Tiger Press 2015
Illustrations copyright © Jill Latter 2015
Jill Latter has asserted her right to be identified as the illustrator
of this work under the Copyright, Designs and Patents Act, 1988

Printers Row Publishing Group is a division of Readerlink Distribution Services,
LLC. The Thunder Bay Press name and logo are trademarks of Readerlink Distribution
Services, LLC.

All notations of errors or omissions should be addressed to Thunder Bay Press,
Editorial Department, at the above address. All other correspondence (author
inquiries, permissions) concerning the content of this book should be addressed to
Little Tiger Press, 1 The Coda Centre, 189 Munster Road, London SW6 6AW

ISBN: 978-1-62686-432-0

Printed in China.
LTP/1800/1389/1215

19 18 17 16 15 2 3 4 5 6

Thank You, Teacher!

THUNDER BAY
P·R·E·S·S
SAN DIEGO

For always *listening* to us, and

helping us find the right answers –

thank you, TEACHER.

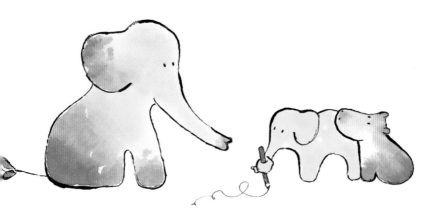

We hope, one day, we'll be just like you –

CLEVER, and *kind,*

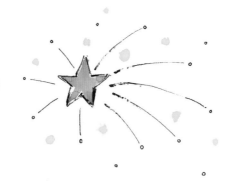

and lots of FUN!

For *always* knowing how to make us laugh –

thank you, TEACHER – you're the BEST!

You make *difficult* things seem so EASY!

We *love* learning from you –

and DISCOVERING new

and *exciting* ideas.

You show us how to make new things,

and HELP us find

the *fun* in anything!

You can do a **MILLION** things – *all* at *once!*

You **EVEN** have eyes in

the back of your head...

you're *our* SUPERHERO teacher!

THANK YOU for always *cheering* us on
to do our *very* BEST!

For staying *patient* when we get things wrong,

for WORKING *late* to grade our papers,

THANK YOU,

lovely teacher!

For **HELPING** us to follow our *dreams* –

thank you, **TEACHER**!

Sometimes we stumble and get things wrong,

but you're ALWAYS there to pick us up.

We *love* the way you get excited when you're

explaining something NEW!

If we feel BLUE, a talk with you makes *everything* BETTER.

For when we *didn't* try our hardest

or LISTEN very well...

we're **SORRY**, teacher!

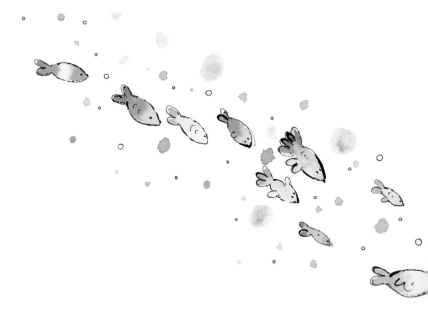

For taking us to *amazing* places,

and showing us so many special things –

THANK YOU!

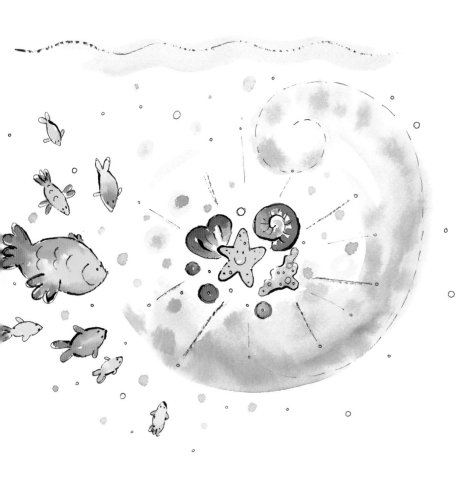

YOU *always* know what to do

when we're STUCK.

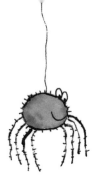

For saying GOOD JOB when we have

tried our hardest –

thank you, TEACHER.

Thank you for helping us use our

IMAGINATIONS to dream up *new* and

wonderful ideas!

To have a **TEACHER** like you makes us so *lucky* –

whatever we do, and *wherever* we go,

we'll **NEVER** forget **YOU!**